Becoming a Person of Mercy

BECOMING A PERSON OF *Mercy*

Personal reflections
and practices on the
WORKS OF MERCY

Max Oliva, SJ

TWENTY-THIRD PUBLICATIONS
twentythirdpublications.com

TWENTY-THIRD PUBLICATIONS
1 Montauk Avenue, Suite 200, New London, CT 06320
(860) 437-3012 » (800) 321-0411 » www.twentythirdpublications.com

ISBN: 978-1-62785-160-2
Library of Congress Catalog Card Number: 2016909027
Printed in the U.S.A.

Contents

Introduction

I am a product of sixteen years of Catholic schooling. My education took place before the Second Vatican Council, when the emphasis was more on God's justice than on God's mercy. Thanks to the Holy Spirit and the wisdom of the Council members, a welcome shift started to happen: toward compassion and "tender mercy" in relation to humanity's moral frailty. Saint John XXIII, at the beginning of the Council, said: "Now the Bride of Christ wishes to use the medicine of mercy rather than taking up arms of severity."

God is the source of mercy. This gives us hope that, with God's help, we too can act mercifully toward others.

In this book, we look at our God of mercy in chapter one. To facilitate our response to God's invitation to be people of mercy, the seven spiritual works of mercy—actions that help our neighbor in their spiritual needs—are presented in chapters two and three. Continuing our response, chapters four and five help us to reflect on the seven corporal works of mercy—those that serve the bodily needs of others. Chapter six addresses Jesus' command that we should love our neighbor as we love ourself by reflecting on how we can be merciful to ourself. Because of the times we live in, it would seem appropriate to have an ad-

ditional work of mercy—our care for the planet on which
we live. Pope Francis' encyclical letter *Laudato Si'* clearly
points us in that direction, and we'll briefly look at that in
the conclusion.

I am indebted to Joe Sinasac of Novalis Publications,
and Therese Ratliff of Twenty-Third Publications, for asking
me to write a book on mercy. This project was inspired by
Pope Francis' declaration of 2016 as a Jubilee Year of Mercy.
I am also grateful to Dan Connors for his excellent editing
of my manuscript.

THE WORKS OF MERCY

The Spiritual Works of Mercy

FORGIVING INJURIES

BEARING WRONGS PATIENTLY

INSTRUCTING THE IGNORANT

ADVISING THE DOUBTFUL

ADMONISHING SINNERS

COMFORTING THE AFFLICTED

PRAYING FOR THE LIVING AND THE DEAD

The Corporal Works of Mercy

FEEDING THE HUNGRY

SHELTERING THE HOMELESS

CLOTHING THE NAKED

GIVING ALMS TO THE POOR

VISITING THE SICK

VISITING THOSE IN PRISON

BURYING THE DEAD

Chapter One

GOD, THE SOURCE OF MERCY

I desire mercy and not sacrifice.
HOSEA 6:6

For the Christian or Jewish believer, the primary source of mercy is God. We find this reality in the Bible, and the place in the Bible where God's mercy is most pronounced is in the covenants.

The four most significant covenants in the Hebrew Scriptures (Old Testament) are the ones between God and Noah, between God and Abraham, between God and Moses, and between God and David. For the purpose of this book, I have chosen the Mosaic covenant as the most meaningful in relation to the mercy of God.

The Book of Exodus is where we see this. In the beginning of the Book of Exodus, we discover that the Israelite people were living as slaves in Egypt. There, the Egyptians oppressed them cruelly (the opposite of mercy) with forced labor. In great distress, the Israelite people cried out to God for help and to free them from this oppression. Into this situation came Moses, who was tending the sheep of his father-in-law when he had an unusual experience. He saw a bush on fire, but the flames were not consuming it. He decided to draw closer to the bush in order to have a better look at this incredible sight.

God then called out to Moses from the bush: "I am the God of your ancestors, the God of Abraham, Isaac, and Jacob" (Exodus 3:6). Then God revealed two particular aspects of the divine personality—compassion and mercy:

> "I have seen how cruelly my people are being treated
> in Egypt; I have heard them cry out to be rescued
> from their slave drivers. I know all about their
> sufferings, and so I have come down to rescue them
> from the Egyptians...." (EXODUS 3:7–8)

Later, when the Israelites grumbled about the harsh conditions on part of their journey toward the Promised Land, God—after Moses pleaded for the people—ceased in his threat to punish them and once again showed them mercy. The author of Psalm 106 sums up this ongoing dynamic:

> Many times the LORD rescued his people...For their
> sake he remembered his covenant, and because of his
> great love he relented. (PSALM 106:43–45)

I am reminded here of Jesus' teaching about how often we should forgive. When Peter asked him, "Lord, if my brother [or sister] keeps on sinning against me, how many times do I have to forgive [them]? Seven times?" "No, not seven times," answered Jesus, "but seventy times seven" (Matthew 18:21–22).

I have to admit that this is a difficult thing for me to do. I have inherited from my Italian father, and likely his father and beyond, a tendency to "write off" people I perceive as seeking to do me harm in some way or another. I remember sharing this with a psychologist friend of mine, who responded: "Very Italian!" Perhaps your culture also struggles with this kind of unlimited mercy. The only solution, in my experience, is to ask God for the grace to let go of whatever ill feeling you have toward the "offending" (in your eyes) person. We will consider this topic again later in the book.

What lies behind the mercy of God is love; for love is the essence of God, as St. John reminds us in his First Letter: "God is love, and those who live in love live in union with God" (4:16). The authors of the *Modern Catholic Encyclopedia* write: "Mercy springs from the passion of love. Love for the other urges both God and God's people to act in kindness and tenderness, to heal and to save."[1]

God's deep concern for humanity is an everlasting mercy,

as Psalm 136 so clearly states. Beginning with the opening sentence, "Give thanks to the Lord for he is good, for his mercy endures forever," all twenty-six verses of the song end with the same refrain: "for his mercy endures forever." God, speaking through the prophet Isaiah, reassures the people of the divine constancy: "Though the mountains leave their place and the hills be shaken, my love shall never leave you nor my covenant of peace be shaken, says the Lord, who has mercy on you" (54:10, NAB).

William Shakespeare captured the true meaning of mercy in *The Merchant of Venice*:

> The quality of mercy is not strain'd.
> It droppeth as the gentle rain from heaven
> Upon the place beneath…
> [Mercy] is enthroned in the hearts of kings,
> It is an attribute to God himself…
> We do pray for mercy;
> And that same prayer doth teach us all to render
> The deeds of mercy."[2]

One of the key characteristics of the mercy of God is "persistence." We see this dynamic especially in the messages of the prophets. Note the following:

Isaiah:
Turn to the LORD and pray to him,
now that he is near.

Let the wicked leave their way of life
and change their way of thinking.
Let them turn to the LORD, our God;
he is merciful and quick to forgive. (55:6–7)

Jeremiah:
[The Lord] told me to go and say to Israel: "Unfaithful
Israel, come back to me. I am merciful and will not be
angry…only admit that you are guilty and that you
have rebelled against the LORD your God." (3:12–13)

Hosea:
Return to the LORD your God, people of Israel. Your
sin has made you stumble and fall." (14:1)

O LORD, you show mercy to those who have no one
else to turn to. (14:3)

The LORD says,
"I will bring my people back to me.
I will love them with all my heart." (14:4)

Micah:
There is no other God like you, O LORD; you forgive
the sins of your people who have survived. You do not
stay angry forever, but you take pleasure in showing us
your constant love. You will be merciful to us once
again. (7:18–19)

These messages of God's love and mercy were a challenge
and a consolation to the people of the time—and to us as
well, for we all depend on the mercy of God.

Many of the psalms, especially those attributed to King
David, are a treasure trove of God's constant love and mercy. Some praise God for protecting the psalmist from his
enemies, such as Psalm 18, which refers to the time David
was rescued from the pursuit of Saul:

> I love you, Lord, my strength,
> Lord, my rock, my fortress, my deliverer.
> My God, my rock of refuge,
> my shield, the horn of my salvation,
> my stronghold! Praised be the Lord, I exclaim,
> and I am safe from my enemies.
> (PSALM 18:1–4, NAB)

This has been an important psalm in my life. God keeps
inviting me to do ministries I never imagined I could do,
ministries that have taken me to places like Northern
Ireland (before the end of the "Troubles") to give retreats
and to South Africa (twice: both times before the end of
Apartheid)—ministries that had me dealing with a fair
amount of fear. I found extra courage in the recitation of
this psalm.

In Psalm 25, the psalmist, again in the voice of David,
acknowledges his need for God's moral guidance and for
mercy:

Turn to me, LORD, and be merciful to me, because I
am lonely and weak.

Consider my distress and suffering and forgive all my
sins. (PSALM 25:16, 18)

Through the prophet Nathan, David sincerely acknowl-
edged his sin in taking another man's wife, Bathsheba, to
be his own while at the same time having her husband
killed (2 Samuel 11—12). Psalm 51 expresses his sorrow:

Be merciful to me, O God,
because of your constant love.
Because of your great mercy
wipe away my sins!
Wash away all my evil
and make me clean from my sin.
(PSALM 51:1–2)

This part of the story of David's life gives us hope. If God
could forgive him for his heinous crimes, how much more
should we trust in God's forgiveness for whatever sins we
have committed![3]
   Psalm 103 praises God for his faithful love and constant
mercy:

Praise the LORD, my soul!
All my being, praise his holy name!

Praise the LORD, my soul,
and do not forget how kind he is.
He forgives all my sins
and heals all my diseases…
and blesses me with love and mercy. (PSALM 103:1–4)

And Psalm 145 extols some of the attributes of God:

The LORD is loving and merciful,
slow to become angry and full of constant love.
He is good to everyone
and has compassion on all he has made.
(PSALM 145:8–9)

Commenting on the proper disposition of those who seek God's help, the psalmist writes:

The Lord is righteous in all he does,
merciful in all his acts.
He is near to those who call to him…
with sincerity. (PSALM 145:17–18)[4]

In the psalms about the mercy of God that are attributed to David, he teaches his readers about the frames of mind and heart they should have toward the Creator: humility, trust, and gratitude. English educator Elizabeth Fry composed the following prayer that summarizes beautifully the sentiments in David's psalm:

Lord, undertake yourself for me;
 Your arm of power can alone heal, help and deliver;
 and in You do I trust, and hope, though at times deeply
  tried and cast down before You;
 yet, O Lord! You are my hope,
 and be therefore entreated of Your poor sorrowful and
  often afflicted servant,
 and arise for my help.
 Leave not my poor soul destitute, but through the
  fullness of Your own power, mercy and love, keep me
 alive unto Yourself, unto the end![5]

In the New Testament, we find many instances of God's mercy.

First of all, Jesus is mercy incarnate, the clearest revelation of God's mercy in the world. We see this in many ways: by his forgiving people of their sins, through his healing ministry, by the manner in which he treats the poor of his day, and by his giving his life for our salvation.

In his encyclical *Rich in Mercy*, Saint John Paul II shares his insights on this reality.

Christ and through Christ, God becomes especially
visible in his mercy; that is to say, there is emphasized
that attribute of the divinity which the Old Testament,
using various concepts and terms, already defined as
"mercy." Christ confers on the whole of the Old
Testament tradition about God's mercy a definitive

meaning. Not only does he speak of it and explain it
by means of comparisons and parables, but above all
he himself makes it incarnate and personifies it. He
himself, in a certain sense, is mercy. To the person who
sees it in him—and finds it in him—God becomes
"visible" in a particular way as the Father "who is rich
in mercy."[6]

Vincent Cardinal Nichols writes, "We look to Christ, who
reveals to us the face of God, the Father of mercies."[7] And
noting the essential role of the Third Person of the Trinity,
he adds, "It is the Holy Spirit who fixes our gaze on Jesus,
who assures us that Jesus' gaze is always upon us, and who
each day makes wonderfully new our relationship with
Jesus."[8]

When we "fix our gaze on Jesus," what do we see? In Pope
Francis' words, we see a man of "tender mercies." My favor-
ite story from Jesus' life that illustrates this description of
Jesus is found in the Gospel of John:

Early the next morning [Jesus] went back to the
Temple. All the people gathered around him, and he
sat down and began to teach them. The teachers of the
Law and the Pharisees brought in a woman who had
been caught committing adultery, and they made her
stand before them all. "Teacher," they said to Jesus, "this
woman was caught in the very act of committing
adultery. In our Law Moses commanded that such a

woman must be stoned to death. Now, what do you say?" They said this to trap Jesus, so that they could accuse him. But he bent over and wrote on the ground with his finger. As they stood there asking him questions, he straightened up and said to them, "Whichever one of you has committed no sin may throw the first stone at her." Then he bent over again and wrote on the ground. When they heard this, they all left, one by one, the older ones first. Jesus was left alone with the woman still standing there. He straightened up and said to her, "Where are they? Is there no one left to condemn you?" "No one, sir," she answered. "Well then," Jesus said, "I do not condemn you either. Go, but do not [do this] sin again."

(JOHN 8:2–11)

In this scene, Jesus takes the humiliation of the woman and turns it into grace for her future. Instead of condemning her, as her accusers wanted, he turns the tables on them while showing her a better way to live. He is a man of "tender mercies."

Commenting on this kind of mercy, Saint John Paul II reminded us of the value of the human person when he wrote that, with Jesus, the person who is the recipient of mercy does not feel humiliated but rather is found again and restored to value.[9]

Second, Jesus is approachable. When the blind beggar Bartimaeus called out to Jesus for help—"Jesus! Son of

David! Have mercy on me!"—the crowd tried to get him to
shut up. Even the disciples were complicit in this scolding.
Jesus stopped and said, "Call him." So they brought him to
Jesus. "What do you want me to do for you?" Jesus asked
Bartimaeus. "Teacher," he replied, "I want to see again." "Go,"
Jesus told him, "your faith has made you well." At once he
received his sight and joined the crowd in following Jesus
(Mark 10:46–52).

When we gaze on Jesus, we see a man who is genuinely
interested in our well-being. Living our faith values on a
daily basis can be a challenge at times, both personally and
professionally. The Lord, in his mercy and compassion, un-
derstands this, and so he says to each of us:

> "Come to me, all of you who are tired from carrying
> heavy loads, and I will give you rest. Take my yoke and
> put it on you, and learn from me, because I am gentle
> and humble in spirit; and you will find rest."
> (MATTHEW 11:28–29)

Take a break to play and to pray. "Be merciful to yourself,"
we hear him say in the silence of our hearts.

If we gaze at Jesus with the same intensity as St. Peter, we
will discover another important aspect of the Lord's mercy:
second chances. Three times Peter denied Jesus, and at a
time when Jesus was in a terrible situation. Here is how
Pope Francis describes the scene: "When [Peter]) hits rock
bottom, he meets the gaze of Jesus who patiently, wordless-

ly, says to him, 'Peter, don't be afraid of your weakness, trust in me.'"[10]

The Apostle Thomas had his own "second-chance" moment as well. Recall the story as it is told by John in chapter 20:24–29. Thomas was not with the other apostles when the risen Christ appeared to them in the room where the Last Supper had taken place. Later, as soon as the others saw Thomas, they excitedly related to him that they had seen the Lord. To which Thomas replied, "Unless I see the scars of the nails in his hands and put my finger on those scars and my hand in his side, I will not believe." A week later, the apostles were once more in the room. This time Thomas was with them. Even though the doors were locked, Jesus appeared again. He looked at Thomas and said to him: "Put your finger here, and look at my hands; then reach out your hand and put it in my side. Stop your doubting and believe!" Thomas answered him, "My Lord and my God!"

Pope Francis shares these thoughts on this story of Thomas:

> How does Jesus react [to Thomas' doubting]? With patience: Jesus does not abandon Thomas in his stubborn unbelief; he gives him a week's time. He does not close the door; he waits. And Thomas acknowledges his own poverty, his little faith: "My Lord and my God!" With this simple yet faith-filled invocation, he responds to Jesus' patience. He lets himself be enveloped by divine mercy.[11]

When we gaze at Jesus, we see his tender mercy, we witness his approachability, we experience his genuine interest in our faith journey, and we are consoled by his merciful patience with our sometimes erring ways.

The Works of Mercy

According to the *Catechism of the Catholic Church*, the works of mercy are charitable actions by which we come to the aid of our neighbor in his or her spiritual and bodily necessities.[12] Moral theologian James F. Keenan adds, "Mercy is the willingness to enter into the chaos of others so as to answer them in their need."[13] There are two categories of the works of mercy: spiritual and corporal. They are listed at the beginning of this book. In the following four chapters we will consider each of these works of mercy in terms of becoming a person of mercy.

FOR REFLECTION
AND DISCUSSION

*Do you have a favorite passage from the Bible, in the
Hebrew Scriptures or the New Testament, that speaks to
you of God's mercy? Why is this passage important for
you?*

_____

_____

_____

_____

_____

_____

*The Lord invites us to live our faith values in both our
personal and professional lives. What helps you to do this?
What hinders you?*

_____

_____

_____

_____

_____

_____

_____

.

Chapter Two

THE SPIRITUAL WORKS OF MERCY, PART I

God is rich in mercy; because of his great love for us, he brought us to life with Christ when we were dead in sin.
EPHESIANS 2:4–5 (NAB)

"I give you a new commandment: love one another. As I have loved you, so you must love one another." JOHN 13:34

Spiritual works of mercy are actions that help our neighbor in his or her spiritual needs. To clear up any possible misunderstanding about the meaning of the word "neighbor," the Fathers of the Second Vatican Council explain: "In our times a special obligation binds us to make ourselves the neighbor of absolutely every person, and of actively helping [them] when [they] come across our path."[1]

To illustrate this truth, allow me to share a story from my own life. In the late 1990s, I moved to a Blackfoot mission in southern Alberta, Canada. This was the first time I had lived among First Nations People. One of the things I learned soon after I arrived was that most of the people who wanted to speak with me privately did not call and make an appointment; they just showed up at my door. At first this annoyed me, until one day when it occurred to me that the person ringing the bell was Jesus—in disguise. That insight caught my attention and changed my attitude. The phrase from a visitor that most put me on alert was, "I am in dire straits!" When I heard those words, I put whatever I was doing aside and just listened to the person in crisis. It was definitely a learning process for me, a lesson in being merciful. The event that convinced me I had grown spiritually happened one late, snowy, winter night. There was a loud banging on my front door. When I opened it, a man was standing there and in need of help. I invited him in. He wanted me to drive him home. I told him I couldn't do it because of the weather. However, I invited him instead to stay overnight in a guest room I had, and I told him that I would drive him home in the morning. He agreed. And that is what happened. I have never forgotten that man or that evening. You see, we helped each other. I helped him by valuing him—in having him as a guest in my home; he helped me to become a better person by giving me the opportunity to serve him in a gracious way.

There are quite a few possible obstacles to being a person of mercy—indifference, judgment, unkindness, prejudice, meanness, cruelty, and hardness of heart. Yet we are called by our faith in Jesus to put on his mind and heart, to be instruments of compassion and caring, kindness and mercy—and, forgiving, as we will see further in this chapter. Jesus tells us to "be merciful just as [God] is merciful" (Luke 6:36).

A profound image from Jesus' passion that bears this out is found in John's gospel. At the foot of the cross after the soldiers had broken the legs of the two men being crucified with Jesus to make sure they were dead, "they saw that [Jesus] was already dead, so they did not break his legs. One of the soldiers, however, plunged his spear into Jesus' side and at once blood and water poured out" (John 19:32–34). The blood and the water are symbols of the love and mercy of Jesus but also of the Father, who gave his Son unto death for our salvation.

Pope Francis reminds us that, as disciples of Jesus, spreading the gospel means that we are the first to proclaim and live the reconciliation, forgiveness, peace, unity, and love that the Holy Spirit gives to us.[2] We are members of the body of Christ, baptized into the community of believers, brothers and sisters in the faith. Mercy is what we owe each other. James F. Keenan adds other motives for being a person of mercy: for the remission of our sins, in gratitude for God's mercy to us, for our prayers to be heard by God, because it leads to eternal reward, and for the sake of the Lord who gave his life for us.[3]

The Fifth Beatitude sums up these opening reflections—"Happy are those who are merciful to others; God will be merciful to them!" (Matthew 5:7).

"Forgiving *as we have been forgiven*"

It is important to begin this section with "As we have been forgiven." I encourage you to think back on your life and how you have experienced God's forgiveness. Speaking from my own life, I remember marveling at God's mercy soon after I entered the Jesuit Novitiate. I was twenty-four years old and had lived a pretty wild life before joining the Jesuits—and yet there I was. Despite my past moral transgressions, God had entered my consciousness and invited me to follow his Son. I was amazed. I still am. The effect on me was amazing too. I decided that if God had this kind of faith in me, I would give my all back to him.

The parable of the prodigal son has helped me to understand what happened to me. Recall the story from Luke 15:11–32. A man had two sons. The younger one asked for his inheritance. So the father divided his property between the two. The younger son then left the family and went to a distant land where he wasted his money in frivolous pursuits. Eventually, he spent everything. A severe famine spread over that land and he was left penniless. So he found a job on a farm where his task was to feed the pigs. At last he came to his senses and, humiliated, decided to return to his father. "I will go to my father," he thought, "and say, 'Father, I have sinned against God and against you. I am no longer fit to be called your son; treat me as one of your hired workers.'" So he left that land and journeyed back to his family. The next scene is one of the most moving in all of Scripture. The younger son "was still a long way from home when his father saw him; his heart was filled with pity and he ran, threw his arms around his son, and kissed him." No judgment, no condemnation! Instead, the father threw a party for him: "Let us celebrate with a feast! For this son of mine was dead, but now he is alive; he was lost, but now he has been found." This is a story about you and me and God. It is as much about the prodigal love of the father as it is of his wayward child. Saint John Paul II eloquently comments on the story:

> Mercy—as Christ presented it in the parable of the prodigal son—has the interior form of the love that in the New Testament is called *agape*. This love is able to reach out to every prodigal son [and daughter], to every human misery, and above all to every form of moral misery, to sin. When this happens, the person who is the object of mercy does not feel humiliated, but rather found again, and restored to value.[4]

Restored to value. Remember the story of the woman accused of adultery, from chapter one? Imagine how she felt when Jesus showed mercy to her! His loving attitude toward her would have changed her life for the better.

Restored to value. Author John Shea has the following interesting reflection on another prominent New Testament figure: Zacchaeus, the tax collector:

> He knows that Jesus is not approving his cheating and graft, but his fundamental created self-worth. Jesus is saying, "Zacchaeus, this heartless thievery is not you. You are more than this!" Jesus does not pound home his sin, but calls to his goodness. Zacchaeus [becomes] who he really is, a created son of the Father, repents, and leads a new life.[5]

Restored to value. My friend Mamie shares this from her faith story: "When I returned to the church and the sacraments after twenty years of rebellion, for several weeks I found myself crying through every Mass that I attended. The tears were mainly tears of joy. I had heard a wonderful homily from a very holy priest that convinced me that I was forgiven for all my many and varied sins." Mamie then became involved in her parish, generously sharing her gifts with the community.

Restored to value. The sacrament of reconciliation is where Roman Catholics have the opportunity to experience a "listening heart" in the confessor, absolution from their sins, and a renewed spiritual and emotional inner harmony. Pope Francis encourages confessors to be "balms of mercy" to penitents. He takes his inspiration from Saint John XXIII, who said that "the Bride of Christ wishes to use the medicine of mercy rather than taking up arms of severity."[6] St. Joseph Cafasso (1811–1860), who was a gifted homilist and merciful confessor, was also the rector (superior) of a seminary in Rome. He encouraged his priests to follow the example of Jesus by being sensitive to the needs of the faithful. "When we hear confessions," he said, "our Lord wants us to be loving and [compassionate], to be fatherly to all who come to us, without reference to who they are or what they have done."[7] Both Saint John XXIII and St. Joseph Cafasso would have taken their cue from this passage in Psalm 103:

> The LORD is merciful and loving,
> slow to become angry and full of constant love.
> He does not keep on rebuking;
> he is not angry forever...
> As high as the sky is above the earth,
> so great is his love for those who honor him.
>
> (PSALM 103:8–11)

As a priest and confessor, I have learned a lot from the confessors I have gone to. The ones I kept (and keep) going back to have certain qualities that I try my best to emulate in the confessional: attentive listening, sensitive questions, and respectful challenging when needed. As a result of my retreat ministry background, I take with me into the confessional a folder of one-page reflections/prayers. When appropriate, I give one of the pages to the penitent for his or her penance. I do this with the penitent's total spiritual life in mind. Some of the themes covered in these handouts are the unconditional love of God, trust in the Lord, dealing with an addiction, and seeking reconciliation with someone. I also have prayers to the Holy Spirit, a prayer for help for those who struggle with engaging in harmful gossiping, a reflection on hope and confidence in God, and a guided meditation on Jesus and the woman at the well (John 4:1–42).

English poet and Anglican priest George Herbert describes in a profound way the love of God and the restoration to value of a sinner. The title of the poem is "Love (III)":

> Love bade me welcome; yet my soul drew back,
> > Guiltie of dust and sinne.
> But quick-ey'd Love, observing me grow slack
> > From my first entrance in,
> Drew nearer to me, sweetly questioning
> > If I lack'd anything.
>
> A guest, I answer'd, worthy to be here:
> > Love said, You shall be he.
> I the unkinde, ungrateful? Ah my deare,
> > I cannot look on thee.
> Love took my hand, and smiling did reply,

> Who made the eyes but I?
> Truth Lord, but I have marr'd them: let my shame
> 　　Go where it doth deserve.
> And know you not, sayes Love, who bore the blame?
> 　　My deare, then I will serve.
> You must sit down, sayes Love, and taste my meat:
> 　　So I did sit and eat.[8]

Forgiving as we have been forgiven

My experience of forgiving another and seeking reconciliation took a radical turn one Palm Sunday. I had decided to sit down and prayerfully read about the Last Supper in order to prepare myself for the upcoming Holy Week. At the time, I was living in a community with twelve other Jesuits at one of our schools of theology. As I reflected on Jesus' extraordinary act of serving his disciples by washing their feet, like a servant would do, I was struck by his words to them after he finished.

> "Do you understand what I have just done to you?…
> You call me Teacher and Lord, and it is right that you
> do so, because that is what I am. I, your Lord and
> Teacher, have just washed your feet. You, then, should
> wash one another's feet. I have set an example for you,
> so that you will do just what I have done for you."
> (JOHN 13:12–15)

What impressed me was that Jesus spoke these words to men

who, in a short while, would either betray or deny him or run and hide for fear of the authorities. This line of thought got me thinking about forgiveness and one of the members of my community. Phil and I had had a falling out about three months earlier. What had originally been some kind of minor misunderstanding had become a major barrier between us, because we hadn't sat down and resolved it. As I read this passage from John's gospel, I asked myself, what would it mean for me to "wash" Phil's feet? The answer came swift and clear: Go talk to him about this rift in your friendship and be reconciled. I hesitated at first, not knowing what Phil's response might be. So I prayed for the courage to take the initiative. This I was able to do.

Phil was a bit wary at first, but as we discerned the root cause of our dispute, he relaxed. We had an excellent sharing and then found it easy to apologize to one another and ask for each other's forgiveness. Reconciliation complete, as a result of God's grace and our willingness to heed it, our friendship was restored.

Five facets of forgiveness
I learned a lot about forgiving another in the above encounter. First of all, as soon as possible after a break in a friendship—after tempers have cooled—it is important to sit down with the other (or do so by phone if the person lives at a distance from you; *never* by e-mail) and discuss the situation. Not to do so is to let the "ant-hill" of disagreement eventually become a "mountain" between the two of

you (as it had become between Phil and me). Also, waiting too long allows pride and resentment to fester. Then there is the added danger of wanting some kind of revenge. Fr. Robert Spitzer, SJ, explains: "Forgiveness is perhaps the most difficult of all virtues because it seeks to temper vengeance, and vengeance always seems justifiable."[9]

Webster's Dictionary defines forgiveness as "to give up resentment against someone or the desire to punish another." My friend Eric, who has been in AA for over forty years, shared with me another negative by-product of resentment: "It is one of the key causes of alcoholism; receiving forgiveness as well as apologizing and making amends to those you have hurt by your addiction are the necessary remedies."

Second, seeking reconciliation demands humility. It involves taking some of the responsibility for the damaged relationship. This applies not only to the root cause of the problem but also, as in my case, letting the unresolved disagreement or hurt linger longer than is reasonable before doing something about it. Theologian Mary E. Hunt comments: "The process of reconciliation sometimes does not get started because people neither realize nor admit that they have caused harm."[10] I may be caught in the "wounded self" syndrome, forgetting that the other person is also feeling wounded. The late spiritual writer Henri Nouwen wrote eloquently about the danger of "clinging to one's wounded self" because it is so self-centered and gets in the way of seeking reconciliation.[11]

Third, I have learned to be careful to not forgive someone prematurely. A part of me wants to get the reconciling over with as soon as possible. This is that part of my personality that doesn't like to "sit with" uncomfortable feelings. But I have to work through my feelings of hurt, possibly even of hate, before I can freely approach the other in a way that does not put her or him immediately on the defensive. The same applies to asking for forgiveness or, for that matter, accepting forgiveness from another. I need to work through my emotions before I can freely ask or receive.

Fourth, there are three dynamics in the area of forgiveness that are important to keep in mind: *forgive and forget, forgive and remember*, and *forgive and go forward*. Sometimes it is easy to *forgive and forget* because the other person is a friend and you do not want any ill feelings to spoil that friendship. I think of this dynamic when reflecting on the story of the father of the prodigal son or that of Jesus and Thomas.

However, what if the other person has an abusive personality? Then *forgive and forget* is not the way to proceed; *forgive and remember* is. I am not thinking of abuse related to children here, but of abuse in adult relationships. I can forgive the abusive person (with the help of God's grace), though it may take some time to get to that point, but I also need to protect myself from future abuse if circumstances are such that I have to stay in personal contact with the person—at my place of work, for example.

I came across the third dynamic from Sister Carolyn Osiek, RSCJ, who wrote, "It is not forgive and forget as if nothing wrong had ever happened, but forgive and go forward, building on the mistakes of the past and the energy generated by reconciliation to create a new future."[12] On the world scene, *forgive and go forward* is what Saint John Paul II did when he went to visit Mehmet Ali Agca, the man who tried to kill him. Here is a description of the event, which took place on December 27, 1983:

> Last week, in an extraordinary moment of grace, the violence in St. Peter's square was transformed. In a bare, white-walled cell in Rome's Rehibbia prison, John Paul tenderly held the hand that had held the gun that was meant to kill him. For 21 minutes, the Pope sat with his would-be assassin. The two talked softly. Once or twice Agca laughed. The Pope forgave him for the shooting. At the end of the meeting, Agca either kissed the Pope's ring or pressed the Pope's hand to his forehead in a Muslim gesture of respect.[13]

Pope John Paul's magnanimous gesture and Agca's respectful response point up a fifth important facet of forgiveness, namely that reconciliation is a "win-win" experience. Both parties are blessed. The forgiver, who has let go of his or her anger and resentment—two toxic emotions associated with hurt—is at peace. For the one forgiven, I will let my favorite author on forgiveness, Lewis B. Smedes, explain:

> What is it like to be forgiven? Forgiveness is

fundamental to every other good feeling…You feel
forgiven at the ground floor of your being, where
everything else rests. It is a feeling of total acceptance,
a feeling lodged in your deepest self…you feel totally
affirmed, totally loved, totally received…This
fundamental feeling happens *to* you. It comes as you
are open to it. You cannot create it; you can only be
receptive to it.[14]

It may happen that the person you are estranged from or
have some unresolved issue with is beyond your reach. This
occurred for a religious sister who was on a six-day retreat I
was presenting to forty sisters. The retreat took place at
their congregation's motherhouse. On the day I shared
some reflections on peacemaking, including the question
about "washing the feet" of someone with whom we are in
conflict, she made an appointment to see me. She told me
that she and another sister in her congregation had had a
disagreement many years before and hadn't spoken to each
other since. I asked her if the other sister was also on the
retreat, and, if so, whether the two of them could find a way
to resolve their differences. She explained that the sister was
indeed on the property but not in the way I imagined. She
was buried in the community cemetery. Later that day, the
sister went to the back of the property, found the gravesite
of the other sister, and engaged in a forgiving prayer exercise. In her imagination, she apologized to the deceased sister and asked for her forgiveness for whatever she had done

to contribute to their falling out. When she came to see me the next day, she described the experience. She felt a great sense of relief and had the feeling that the other sister had forgiven her too.

In all things, it helps to have a forgiving attitude and a desire to be to others as God is to us: loving, compassionate, patient, slow to anger, and merciful. Again, Jesus gives us a goal in the Fifth Beatitude: "Happy are those who are merciful to others; God will be merciful to them!" (Matthew 5:7). And St. Paul gives us the direction:

> God has reconciled us to himself through Christ and
> has given us the ministry of reconciliation. I mean that
> God, in Christ, was reconciling the world to himself
> not counting [our] transgressions against [us], and
> that he has entrusted the ministry of reconciliation to
> us. That makes us ambassadors for Christ, God as it
> were appealing through us. (2 CORINTHIANS 5:14–20,
> NAB)

FOR REFLECTION
AND DISCUSSION

God asks us to "love our neighbor as [we love] ourself."
Are there any people in your life whom you find difficult
to love? What would it mean to "wash their feet"?

_____

_____

_____

_____

_____

_____

_____

_____

Chapter Three

THE SPIRITUAL WORKS OF MERCY
PART II

Bearing Wrongs Patiently

"You have heard that it was said, 'An eye for an eye, and a tooth for a tooth. But now I tell you: do not take revenge on someone who wrongs you." MATTHEW 5:38

Patience is not my strongest virtue. Neither is tolerance for being treated unjustly. Being falsely accused, being treated unfairly, even slandered, invokes in me a deep desire to right the wrong immediately and set those responsible straight and in no uncertain terms. Writer Mark Shea, in his insightful article "Bear Wrongs Patiently," has a reaction similar to my own (and perhaps to yours as well):

> Generally, my reaction to those who sin against me
> and against those I love is to grind my teeth and take
> walks or showers where I formulate the Perfect
> Riposte to That Jerk…On my weaker days, I let fly
> with words calculated to hurt. On my stronger days, I
> simply stew in my juices and have to work long and
> hard to really hand those people over to God and ask
> that they be forgiven.[1]

Bearing wrongs patiently is hard. It takes discipline and a lot of grace from God. I am reminded of this admonition every time I recite these words of the Lord's Prayer, "forgive us our trespasses as we forgive those who trespass against us."

It also helps to have a hero or heroine who inspires you to live this spiritual work of mercy. Mine is Jackie Robinson, No. 42, the great African American baseball player who changed American society by ending racial segregation in the major leagues.

I owe the following remarks to another baseball great, Steve Garvey.[2] Jackie, who was born in Cairo, Georgia, in 1919, was the grandson of a slave and the son of a sharecropper. The team that signed him was the Brooklyn Dodgers. Branch Rickey, the Dodgers innovative and courageous general manager and president, had decided to break baseball's color barrier. Rickey had searched for the right player to help him accomplish his dream; he thoroughly investigated

Robinson's background, character, and reputation, and chose him. Here is Steve Garvey on the initial meeting that took place between Rickey and Robinson:

> Rickey explained to Robinson that what they were about to embark on was much greater than baseball. And the resistance they would face would be fierce. Rickey told Robinson he knew he would be a good enough ballplayer, what he didn't know was whether he had the "guts" to endure the hatred he would face, "no matter what happens."[3]

Robinson was twenty-six years old at the time. He said much later that since he had been eight years old and experienced his first encounter with a racist person, his attitude had been retaliation and payback as a way to protect his personal dignity. When Rickey proposed his plan to him, Robinson asked him if he was looking for a ballplayer who was afraid to fight back. "Robinson," Rickey replied forcefully, "I am looking for a ballplayer with guts enough not to fight back!"

Prejudice and bigotry were their constant companions. In the beginning, Jackie endured intense abuse even from players on other teams. After one particularly difficult game, Jackie said that torment from trying to ignore the insults nearly sent him over the edge. But then he remembered Rickey's admonition and took it.

Robinson would later write:

I started the season as a lonely man, often feeling like a
black Don Quixote tilting at a lot of white windmills.
I ended up feeling like a member of a solid team…I
had learned how to exercise self-control—to answer
insults, violence, and injustice with silence—and I had
learned how to earn the respect of my teammates.
They had learned that it's not skin color but talent
and ability that counts.[4]

Teammate Duke Snider said of Robinson, "Jackie made us
better because of his ability, and he made us closer as a
team because of his suffering."

How like Christ! The prophet Isaiah, in one of the four
servant-of-the-Lord oracles, each of which points to fulfill-
ment in Jesus, proclaims: "It was our infirmities that he
bore, our sufferings that he endured…Though he was
harshly treated, he submitted and opened not his mouth"
(Isaiah 53:4, 7, NAB).

Jesus and Jackie—these are my two go-to heroes who
inspire me when I am faced with a challenge to bear
wrongs patiently. Who are your heroes? Your heroines?

Instructing the Ignorant
Advising the Doubtful

Jesus said to Peter: "Take care of my lambs…
Take care of my sheep." John 21:15–16

In terms of faith and morals, we were all "ignorant" in the beginning. We needed competent and committed teachers to show us the way. For some of us, baptism happened early in life; for others, in adulthood. I am deeply grateful to my parents for having me baptized as a baby and for sending me to a Catholic elementary school and a Jesuit high school. My mother and father introduced me to the basics of the faith and various spiritual practices, like the Mass, the Rosary, grace at meals, and prayers before going to sleep. I am grateful as well for the sisters who taught me about the Bible and how our religion is centered on the person of Jesus. In high school, the faith formation of my earlier years was deepened through the religion classes I took and through the quality of my teachers. They instructed me in a non-condescending way, perhaps because they too realized they had risen from ignorance to knowledge. I was fortunate enough to attend a Catholic university, which expanded what I had learned about our faith in high school and introduced me to a broader look at societal moral issues in terms of faith. Each step of the way, a new level of knowledge erased an earlier level of ignorance. I was the one being instructed!

At the age of twenty-four, I came to the realization that I

have a vocation. I had graduated from college and traveled in Europe for four months shortly after graduation—which gave me a more comprehensive understanding of world issues; for example, I was in Berlin eight days after the wall went up. Upon returning home, I enlisted in the United States Coast Guard in a special program for college graduates: six months active duty and seven and a half years in the reserves; this gave me both a chance to learn a new level of discipline and the opportunity to meet men from many different backgrounds.

Work-wise, my plan had been to work in the food industry for a couple of years and then join my father in his food brokerage company. So I went to work for a food cannery as a salesman. There I received a different kind of education as I encountered some very upstanding businessmen and women and a few with a non-ethical orientation; the main transgression was the padding of expense accounts by some of the other salesmen.[5]

Joining the Jesuits, in my mid-twenties, was the best decision of my life. I was introduced to ways of praying that I had not known about, like using my imagination to meditate on a passage with Jesus in it. This helped me immensely to get to know him as a person and as a companion on the journey.[6] My image of God shifted from one of judgment to one of mercy. This led to a reappraisal of my self-image—from a low one, judged by the sins of my past and putting my self-worth in what I had owned before entering the Novitiate (first two years of Jesuit training), to the unconditional love of God as the foundation of my identity. Rising from a kind of naive ignorance to spiritual wisdom was a gradual process aided in large part by some remarkable Jesuit mentors.

Midway through my formation process to ordination (I was on the "short course": nine years!), I was sent to live in a black, inner-city parish in San Francisco. This was during the civil rights struggle of the 1960s. There I was to become a "novice" again, this time in terms of my social conscience—how one relates to the social issues of one's time and of social grace and social sin.[7]

Before moving to the parish mentioned above, I had read James Baldwin's powerful book *The Fire Next Time* and Richard Wright's masterpiece, *Native Son*. These two books gave me the philosophical background to the issue of race relations in the US. The ministry I became engaged in—securing job interviews for African American men who were out of work (and some of whom had arrest records)—put me in direct contact with the community on the streets, in pool halls, and in other public gathering places.

As people got to know me, they started to educate me. They did this mainly by sharing their personal stories of discrimination and exclusion from the wider society. As a result of these disclosures, I began to have what I call a "conversion to compassion" experience. The first step in this dynamic of conversion for me was to listen attentively to the stories. The second was to admit to myself that I had certain prejudices about black people. The third step was to discover the falsity of my assumptions. The great spiritual writer Henri Nouwen has a similar insight: "Compassion asks us to go where it hurts, to enter into places of pain, to share in brokenness, fear, confusion, and anguish. Compassion challenges us to cry out with those in misery, to mourn with those who are lonely, to weep with those in tears."[8] In the years since, I have had a number of "conversion to compassion" experiences.[9]

As for *Advising the Doubtful*, one need go no further than Thomas the Apostle. Jesus not only gave him a second chance, he gave him a week to mull over what the other Apostles had told him. Author Frederick Buechner, in his book *Peculiar Treasures*, describes the scene well:

> [A week] later, when Jesus did come back, Thomas was there and got his wish. Jesus let him see him and hear him and touch him, and not even Thomas could hold out against evidence like that. He had no questions left to ask and not enough energy left to ask them with even if he'd had a couple. All he could say was, "My Lord and my God!" (John 20:28), and Jesus seemed to consider that under the circumstances that was enough.[10]

Certainly, sensitivity to the doubtful one is necessary so he or she will not feel rejected—sensitivity and the "balm of mercy."

Admonishing Sinners

I, the Lord, am a God who is full of compassion, who is not easily angered and who shows great love and faithfulness. Exodus 34:6

Two of the things I like about Pope Francis are his emphasis on mercy rather than judgment and condemnation and his invitation to those who are doubtful or errant in their faith. He takes his cues from the passage quoted above from the Book of Exodus and from the following words of Saint John XXIII as he opened the Second Vatican Council, "Now the Bride of Christ wishes to use the medicine of mercy rather than taking up arms of severity." Then, speaking of the church's separated brothers and sisters, Saint John said, "The Catholic Church wants at this Council to show herself a loving mother to all; patient, kind, moved by compassion and goodness."[11]

Both popes, no doubt, had St. Peter in mind—he, of the "denying," when Jesus needed him most. And yet Jesus appointed him the first head of the church (Matthew 16:18).

Here is Pope Francis reflecting on Jesus' manner:

> Jesus, the Good Shepherd, does not humiliate or
> abandon people to remorse. Through him the
> tenderness of the Father, who consoles and revitalizes,
> speaks; it is he who brings us from the disintegration
> of shame—because shame truly breaks us up—to the
> fabric of trust. He restores courage, reconstructs
> responsibility, and sends us out on mission."[12]

This is certainly my story. And I am sure the reader can relate as well. Regardless of my past moral transgressions, God invited me to be a priest! This reality continues to amaze me. We will revisit "admonishing the sinner" in chapter four when we consider the first of the corporal works of mercy.

Comforting the Afflicted

When evening came, people brought to Jesus many who had demons in them. Jesus drove out the evil spirits with a word and healed all who were sick. MATTHEW 8:16

In the gospels, we see many different kinds of afflictions. There are people blind from birth, lepers, some who were mute, and those possessed by demons. There is the paralytic in the town of Capernaum (Mark 2:1–12), a woman with a hemorrhage who had been suffering for a dozen years (Mark 5:25–34), and the servant of a centurion near death (Luke 7:1–10). Regardless of the affliction, Jesus was present to each person. St. Matthew expresses it well:

> Jesus left there [the territory near the cities of Tyre and Sidon] and went along by Lake Galilee. He climbed a hill and sat down. Large crowds came to him, bringing with them the lame, the blind, the crippled, the [mute], and many other sick people, whom they placed at Jesus' feet; and he healed them. (MATTHEW 15:29–30)

In another scene, Jesus and his disciples went off in a boat by themselves for some rest from the crowds, but the people found out where they were going and arrived there by land before Jesus did. St. Mark describes the situation: "When Jesus got out of the boat he saw this large crowd, and his heart was filled with pity for them, because they were like sheep without a shepherd" (Mark 6:34).

Jesus displays four impressive qualities in his healing ministry: first, *his approachability*—people with all kinds of ailments came to him entrusting to him their wounds and asking for his help; second, *his lack of fear* in touching those he healed, even lepers (Luke 4:40); third, *his availability* as he walked with his disciples in public places and in the countryside; and fourth, *his compassion*.

Compassion, which is essential in comforting the afflicted—be the problem physical, emotional, mental, or spiritual—is often expressed in a stance of presence. In the 1980s, Karen Jaenke wrote an insightful article on ministering to those with AIDS. She said at one point:

> AIDS confronts us with an enormous sense of
> helplessness. Most of us are result-oriented, like to see
> tangibles, need external confirmation. AIDS gives very
> little of that...if one is to endure in this ministry, it
> must be grounded on some other basis...For me, this
> basis is presence. I refer to an *accepting presence*
> [emphasis added], also called unconditional love.[13]

Jesus is the consummate example of "accepting presence."
We witness this in a special way in the story of the penitent
woman as related by St. Luke:

> There was a certain Pharisee who invited Jesus to dine
> with him. Jesus went to the Pharisee's home and
> reclined to eat. A woman known in the town to be a
> sinner learned that he was dining in the Pharisee's
> home. She brought in a vase of perfumed oil and
> stood behind him at his feet, weeping so that her tears
> fell upon his feet. Then she wiped them with her hair,
> kissing them and perfuming them with oil.
>
> (LUKE 7:36–38, NAB)

Jesus does not push the woman away out of embarrassment
or fear of what his host might think. He lets her wash his
feet and then publicly forgives her sins. He accepts her as
she is and gives her the gift of mercy.

The gift of mercy can also be seen in a different light
from Phyllis Rodriguez, whose son, Gregory, was killed in
the terrorist attack on the Twin Towers on September 11,
2001. Remarkably, Phyllis later befriended Aicha el-Wafi,
the mother of the 9/11 conspirator Zacarias Moussaoui.
Writer Angela Alaimo O'Donnell tells the story:

> The sight of another mother's suffering as her son is
> arrested, tried, and threatened with the death
> penalty—and remembering her own son's youthful

rebelliousness and episodes of poor judgment—[led]
Phyllis to seek out the mother of her supposed enemy
and stand in solidarity with her. Both Phyllis and her
husband, Orlando, eventually testified at Moussaoui's
trial, playing a decisive role in the court's decision to
spare his life.[14]

There are numerous afflictions in the world today. On a
personal level, there are terminal illnesses, mental illnesses,
people who are developmentally disabled, elders who have
been abandoned by their relatives, to name a few.

Two people who, on a personal level, exemplify "comforting the afflicted," or receiving comfort, are Carl and
Mimi Smith. In his heartwarming book, *Special Love*, Carl
tells the story of their son Carlton, who was born in 1959
with severe Down Syndrome.[15] It's a story of the special
love that Carlton gave, received, and spread to his mother
and father, his brother and two sisters, his extended family,
and all the people who came into his life. It's difficult to say
who the afflicted are in this story. Was it Carlton? Was it his
parents? His siblings? Certainly, in the early years of
Carlton's life, Carl and Mimi were afflicted with uncertain-
ty about how to raise their child. At the time of his childhood, not a lot was known about persons with severe
Down Syndrome. Carl relates how God providentially put
dedicated people in their lives to comfort and educate him
and Mimi. And how, over the years, medical and behavioral
sciences have made enormous progress in understanding

people who are developmentally disabled. Indeed, comfort can come from a variety of sources.

On a societal level, the person who immediately comes to my mind as one who comforts many and well is Kathleen Miller. Kathleen is the founder and Executive Director of Living Grace Home, a safe haven for expectant teenage mothers in Las Vegas, Nevada. Most of the young moms come from difficult economic, social, and family situations. Kathleen and her staff are committed to giving homeless and pregnant youth a sense of hope, a sense of opportunity, and a sense that anything is possible. Living Grace Home offers comfort to these young women and their babies by providing a safe living environment as well as programs and support for their emotional and spiritual development. The staff also helps the young moms to learn new skills in order to become more independent.

Pope Francis is one of the major actors in the work of comforting the afflicted on a global scale. In an informative article titled "The Migrant Pope," author J. Kevin Appleby relates how the pope's focus on migrants and refugees is bearing fruit both in Europe and in the United States. During his trip to Lampedusa, Italy, the closest European soil for the landing of boats carrying thousands of migrants seeking asylum in Europe, he celebrated Mass to remember the hundreds of migrants who have died trying to reach a new home. Mr. Appleby writes:

In addition to his visit to Lampedusa, the pope has skillfully combined his words with small but profound acts of compassion toward forced migrants and solidarity with them, thus amplifying his message. He has had Christmas gifts delivered to residents of a migrant shelter near the Vatican, visited a Jesuit-run refugee shelter in Rome, and more recently, sent Easter cakes to Christian refugees in Iraq.[16]

Pope Francis has shows a keen interest in the U.S.-Mexico border. He wrote a letter to the Mexico/Holy See Colloquium on Migration and Development, held in Mexico City in July 2014, calling for the comfort and protection of unaccompanied children fleeing violence in Central America.

What is the main message of the pope's firm defense of immigrants and refugees? Appleby comments: "It is that these persons are our brothers and sisters and should be afforded the same rights as all of God's children—to live their lives in safety and with the opportunity to reach their God-given potential."[17]

The pope, along with all the other men and women involved in this spiritual act of mercy—comforting the afflicted—bring love and hope to those in need. Each has responded positively to God's grace; each is an inspiration to us all.

Praying for the Living and the Dead

I am a product of the pre-Vatican II church. We learned in childhood about our soul going to a "place" or "state" after death called Purgatory. According to the *Catechism of the Catholic Church*, Purgatory is the final purification before entering heaven. In section 1030 of the *Catechism* we read: "All who die in God's grace and friendship, but still imperfectly purified, are indeed assured of their eternal salvation; but after death they undergo purification, so as to achieve the holiness necessary to enter the joy of heaven."

When I was growing up, my parents and the religious sisters at elementary school taught us to pray regularly for the souls in Purgatory, whether we had known them before they died or not. It is one way we have of honoring them. I frequently pray for my deceased relatives—as well as my living ones.

My first experience of the death of someone close to me was the death of my mother. She struggled with cancer for two years before she died at the age of forty-six. I was twenty; my sisters were thirteen, eleven, and five, and my brother was three. My mother had an amazing faith; she trusted completely in the providence of God to take care of my dad and her children. Grief over her death hit me in "waves." But this was nothing compared to what my dad suffered and what my mother's mother suffered. My grandmother lost two of her four children and her husband before she died. Both my mother and my grandmother had a devotion to our Blessed Mother, so when I read the following story from author Ann Dawson about the death of her eighteen-year-old son, the third of her four children, I couldn't help but think of our family. Perhaps her story will resonate with you in some way. Mrs. Dawson begins her story with a quote from Luke 2:34–35: "Simeon said to Mary, [Jesus'] mother, 'And sorrow, like a sharp sword, will break your own heart.'"

> On the morning of Andy's death, I was overcome by a sudden urge to get outside of the hospital for a few moments. As I walked outside, I saw in front of me a gate leading to a fenced-in yard. I went through the gate and as I rounded a corner, I saw directly in front of me a large sculpture of the crucifixion, with life-sized statues of Jesus on the cross and his mother Mary beneath him. It was as if I had been led to this place. I sat on the ground at Mary's feet. And for a moment, I became the woman beneath the cross. I went back in time 2000 years and felt the unbearable pain of watching a beloved son suffer an unbelievably hideous death. I felt the abandonment, the despair, and the fear of that good woman. And I knew then that she was with me at that moment. She held me and wept for me and for all mothers who had to bury a child. She knew my pain. She had come to experience the words of Simeon's prophecy, but she had also experienced the resurrection. She is the hope of all beloved mothers, and all those who know the pain of losing a loved one.[18]

At the time of this writing, I had just received the news that one of my dearest friends, Ernie McCullough, had died. He was ninety years old. Ernie was not only a good friend but also a mentor to me. I shall deeply miss our visits. In the spirit of praying for the living and the dead, I pray for him on his final journey, and I pray for his wife, Sue, and all the McCullough family as they continue to grieve the loss of this remarkable man.

In addition to praying for those who have died, I keep a "prayer list" of requests from friends for everything from a surgery coming up to starting a new job. I truly believe in the power of prayer because I have seen its salutary effects in my own life as well as in the lives of others. When I read about some terrible atrocity in the world, I often spontaneously ask God to take those killed to himself and to comfort their loved ones. And I pray, when I have the grace, for those who did the evil, for their conversion; this is the most difficult group to pray for—until I remember Jesus' words from the cross: "Forgive them, Father! They don't know what they are doing" (Luke 23:34).

To conclude this spiritual work of mercy and this chapter, I want to share a letter sent to me and to others who expressed their sympathy to one of my Jesuit brothers on the death of his mother. He expresses profoundly the meaning of "praying for the living and the dead" and all of its implications.

Please know how grateful I am for your kind and generous expressions of sympathy at the death of my beloved mother. Words cannot possibly express the depth of my appreciation for your good thoughts and kind prayers at the most difficult and disorienting time of my life. Let me assure you that I have felt your support and love reaching across time and space, holding me up so that I might stay present to the realities before me and remain alert to the mysterious workings of God's grace. How can I possibly thank you for such a gift? I pray that you may feel the Holy Spirit, the Advocate, within and around you, assuring you that where there is Love there is God, and Love is always stronger than death.

FOR REFLECTION
AND DISCUSSION

Think about each of the spiritual works of mercy:

Bearing Wrongs Patiently: *Have you had an experience where you felt you were treated unjustly? If so, how did you react?*

Instructing the Ignorant: *What are some of the key life lessons you have learned that have helped you to become a better person?*

Advising the Doubtful: *How would you respond to someone who is struggling with his or her faith?*

Admonishing Sinners: *What virtues do you think are needed to call another to conversion?*

Comforting the Afflicted: *What passage from Jesus' life most clearly speaks to you of his compassion for the afflicted?*

Praying for the Living and the Dead: *How do you feel about praying for the conversion of criminals and terrorists as well as family members and friends?*

Chapter Four

THE CORPORAL WORKS OF MERCY PART I

> *Jesus left there and went along by Lake Galilee. He climbed a hill and sat down. Large crowds came to him, bringing with them the lame, the blind, the crippled, the [mute], and many other sick people, whom they placed at Jesus' feet; and he healed them.* MATTHEW 15:29–30

One of the definitions of mercy, as presented in the Merriam-Webster Dictionary, is: "compassionate treatment of those in distress, for example, works of mercy among the poor." "Those in distress" brings to mind the parable of the good Samaritan (Luke 10:25–37). A Jewish man is on his way to the city of Jericho from Jerusalem. On his journey, he is set upon by thieves who rob him, beat him up, and leave him half dead. Three people see him lying in the road, two, a priest and a Levite, pass by without stopping, while the third, a Samaritan, tends to the victim's needs, and helps him get back on his feet. To pious Jews in Jesus' time, the term "Samaritan" had very negative connotations. Samaritans were detested even more than pagans. The story Jesus tells is occasioned by a Jewish lawyer who knows that to inherit eternal life he is to love God with all his heart and his neighbor as himself. But wanting to justify himself, he asks Jesus, "Who is my neighbor?"

Each of the characters in the story, but especially the Samaritan, the priest, and the Levite (these were assistants to the priests) represent not only a role but, more important, an attitude. The priest and the Levite ignore the man. The Samaritan not only acts with compassion, but goes beyond simple charity to provide for the man's recovery. He is the true observer of God's Law, because he places love above all other considerations.

The parable of the good Samaritan gives us a chance to be inspired by the actions of the Samaritan while at the same time considering what may blind us in our own day to the plight of the poor and those in distress for any reason (the reader will note that some of these are mentioned in chapter two on the spiritual works of mercy). Consider the following possible obstacles:

A legalistic mentality that lets the law trump love, unlike the Arizona rancher who, finding bodies of migrants on his ranch, sets out water and other supplies so they can complete their journey safely, or the organization Los Samaritanos, which also leaves water and food along well-known foot trails; they say they are doing moral deeds in the face of a simple reality: migrants keep coming despite the legal issues.

A judgmental attitude that claims, for example, that people who are economically poor are lazy and just want to be on welfare.

Indifference to the plight of others or lack of an "understanding heart."

Ignorance, sometimes the result of a lifestyle that insulates one from the hardships of others.

As followers of Christ, we are called to reach out mercifully to others just as we have been compassionately treated by God. In Psalm 146, we discover some of the key attributes of the Creator: "[God] always keeps his promises; he judges in favor of the oppressed and gives food to the hungry. The LORD sets prisoners free and gives sight to the blind…He protects the strangers who live in our land; he helps widows and orphans" (Psalm 146:6–9).

In this chapter and in the next, we will consider the

seven corporal works of mercy: feeding the hungry, sheltering the homeless, clothing the naked, visiting the sick, visiting those in prison, giving alms to the poor, and burying the dead.

Feeding the Hungry

Love Jesus in all his distressing disguises.
BLESSED MOTHER TERESA OF CALCUTTA

Jesus is the prime model for living this corporal work of mercy. We see in Matthew's gospel Jesus' concern for those who are hungry. A large crowd had assembled to hear him preach. He said to his disciples: "I feel sorry for these people, because they have been with me for three days and now have nothing to eat. I don't want to send them away without feeding them, for they might faint on their way home" (Matthew 15:32).[1] This leads, as we know, to the miracle of the "seven loaves" and "a few small fish"—for "all ate and had enough" and there were even leftovers.

Where did Jesus get this sensitivity to the needs of others? Who influenced him to be a person of compassion? His mother, it seems to me. Mary, "comforter of the afflicted," the Virgin of Guadalupe who reached out to the poor of Mexico, of whom St. Ephrem wrote, "[She] is the comfort of the world, the mother of orphans, the liberator of prisoners, and the redeemer of captives."

Who influenced you to be a person of compassion?

Whose example has inspired you to reach out to those wounded by hunger and oppression? Who inspires you now?

As a Jesuit, I have been privileged to live and work among African Americans in an inner city, among Mexican people in Tijuana, Mexico, and among a First Nations community in Alberta, Canada.[2] And I lived for a summer in Calcutta, India.[3] I trace the roots of my concern for the economic struggles of others to my mother and, indirectly, to my father. My dad was a food broker. Once or twice a week, he would bring home samples of food, which he would place in a cupboard. His idea of family was us: himself, my mom, my three sisters, my brother, and me. My mother's idea of family, however, was anyone in town in need—someone recommended by our parish's St. Vincent de Paul Society, a little Spanish parish in the town next to ours, and the cloistered Carmelite sisters who depended on the goodness of others for food. As you can imagine, these two views of "family" caused some interesting interchanges between my parents at times!

"Feeding the hungry" often takes us out of our comfort zone. In his book *The Church of Mercy*, Pope Francis asks us not to be afraid to go to the "furthest boundaries and outskirts of human existence to meet the poor, the marginalized, and the least" of our brothers and sisters.[4] It is the Holy Spirit who makes it possible for us to take this risk. Pope Francis urges us to move past our fear and to go into new territories of poverty and want: "God is always pushing, pushing forward. God is not afraid of the outskirts. If you go to the outskirts, you will find him there. God is always faithful and creative."[5] As many have experienced, going out of oneself brings untold blessings from those whom we seek to serve.

Certainly, this has been my experience. Whether you help out at a soup kitchen, in a Meals on Wheels program, at a refugee camp, or with some other program, you will find Jesus there in one of his distressing disguises.

One small, but very personal action I do whenever I am driving is greet street people who beg at intersections; I carry in my car a box of power bars and give two to each person with an as-audible-as-possible "God bless you." Often their thanks and "God bless you" to me is said before I get mine out.

In addition to feeding the body, this work of mercy can be applied to "feeding the mind." Someone who has become an effective practitioner of "feeding the mind" is Ed Bevilacqua.

Ed is a college graduate and has a law degree. He was a successful businessman in a competitive industry before he was charged and sentenced for securities fraud. Married and the father of six children, he was arrested at his home and then spent three years of incarceration. He told me that his goal was to come out of prison better spiritually, mentally, emotionally, and physically. While serving his time, he regularly attended whatever religious services were offered. During his third year in prison, he spent two weeks in solitary confinement in a seven- by ten-foot cell. "It was a crucible of my soul," he said. Without books to read, the ability to write, or a television to watch, he discovered the way to keep his sanity was to use his memory and imagination. He said,

> I remembered part of a poem that helped me to make sense of the situation: "Stone walls do not a prison make, nor iron bars a cage. Minds innocent and quiet, take [this] as a hermitage."[6] Solitary became a place where I could follow my imagination and focus my attention on what I wanted to do once I was released from prison. You see, my time in prison, and in solitary, made me a person of mercy as I gained a new perspective on humanity. I grew up believing that if a person worked hard they could do anything they wanted in life, and those who were not successful were that way because they didn't want to put in the necessary effort to be so. But in prison, I discovered that most of my fellow inmates grew up believing a completely different worldview; they were told that nothing was possible and anything they earned would be taken away from them, so why bother? Once I realized that, it changed everything for me, and I determined to do whatever I could once I was released to help those coming out of prison to change that way of thinking.

Ed chose education as the way to accomplish this. With the help of a benefactor, Ed became the Director of Education for Larson Training Center in Las Vegas, Nevada, a vocational school for adult learners, most of whom have spent some time in jail. Larson Training Center has the distinction of having the highest placement rate in the state (87%). Each session there lasts sixteen weeks. Basic skills for applying for and securing employment are taught in a supportive atmosphere. "If you feed the mind, you feed the soul, and the world will be the better for it," might be the motto of this model of merciful love.

Sheltering the Homeless

Give me courage to serve others, for in service there is true life.
CESAR CHAVEZ

According to Urban Institute of the organization Future in Humanity, homelessness in the United States is a "revolving door" crisis. Many people exit homelessness quickly, but many more become homeless every day. On any given day, at least 800,000 people are homeless, including about 200,000 children in homeless families.[7] The main causes are mental disabilities, domestic abuse, job loss, and the high cost of housing in many large cities that is more than even many of the working poor can afford.

Consider the following two stories. One is from a woman called "Jane," a college graduate but the victim of domestic violence, and the other is from a couple who went out of their way to assist a woman with mental illness. Here is Jane's account of her struggle.

> At the lowest point in my life, I had to seek a roof over my head at a homeless shelter for women and children. This was a situation I had never envisaged myself to be in, having been financially secure for well over twenty years. At the shelter I was warmly received and given some basic necessities: a washcloth, toothbrush and toothpaste, and soap. I remember sobbing uncontrollably. The women at the shelter may not realize how their little acts of kindness impacted me and helped me to continue on my journey. Years later, I still have the washcloth as a reminder that even in my darkest hour there will always be someone there to hold me and comfort me—because God will never abandon me.

The shelter that Jane stayed at is called The Shade Tree. The Shade Tree's statements of belief are:

• That no one should ever have to endure a state of homelessness, existing in fear for personal safety and without the means to meet even the most basic of human needs—food and shelter.

- That every human being, regardless of social status, has the right to be treated with dignity and respect.

- That all homeless children are victims because they lack choice and mobility.

- That homelessness is a community problem that impacts everyone.

- That everyone can be a part of the solution.

Listening to Jane tell her story radically improved my understanding of some of the devastating effects of violence in a home.

The second story comes from a married couple, friends of mine for many years. They live in a semirural town located in San Diego County. Here is their story as related by the husband.

> One evening, as I was driving to pick up a pizza at our neighborhood pizza parlor, an elderly lady approached my truck. She was in a very agitated state. She told me her name was "Jan." She complained that the low-rent apartment where she lived was plagued by constant loud music from some of the other apartments; when she complained, the people played it all the louder. While trying to calm her down, I thought of our empty little studio apartment behind our house. I

invited her to come and see it. She did and liked it. We moved her in, and she lived there for many years, until she died, in fact. After a while, we discovered that Jan was mentally ill. She was alienated from her three children, whom we never met. Occasionally, she would hurl insults at some of our friends. In short, she was not an easy person to have on our property, yet we felt she needed us.

I live in Las Vegas, Nevada. Partly because of the weather, people are drawn to live here. Not all do well financially. For those who are in need, there are excellent resources, such as soup kitchens that serve street people and the working poor, organizations that provide overnight accommodation to those who are homeless, resources for women and children who are fleeing domestic violence, and programs to reach homeless youth with a safe place to stay and the opportunity for education.

Clothing the Naked

"I was hungry and you fed me, thirsty and you gave me a drink… naked and you clothed me." MATTHEW 25:35–36

For Christians, the most tragic example of "being stripped naked" is Jesus on the cross. After Pilate handed Jesus over to be crucified, his tormentors took off his clothes and dressed him in royal purple and wove a crown of thorns and put it on his head; and mocking him they began to salute him: "Long live the King of the Jews!" (Mark 15:16–18). Mark Shea notes that "to nake someone, to strip them publicly, is universally understood as taking away their human dignity. Clothes, in some mystical sense, quite literally make the [person]."[8] After Jesus died, the first visible sign that his dignity was being restored came at the hands of a wealthy disciple of his—Joseph of Arimathea. St. Matthew takes it up from there: Joseph "went into the presence of Pilate and asked for the body of Jesus. Pilate gave orders for the body to be given to [him]. So Joseph took it, wrapped it in *a new linen sheet* [emphasis mine], and placed it in his own tomb, which he had just recently dug out of solid rock" (Matthew 27:57–60).

Joseph's generous gestures are definitely corporal works of mercy. Over the centuries since the death of Jesus, thousands of men and women, lay, clergy, and religious, have responded generously to Jesus' call "to love your neighbor as you love yourself" (Mark 12:31), which finds clear expression in the corporal works of mercy. Here are some practical ways to live "clothing the naked":

- At home, go through your clothes closets and find clothing that could be donated for the good of others; make sure the items are clean and wearable.

- Donate your time and energy to a local thrift shop, making sure you get a chance to meet the people who come in and greeting them as if they were a long-lost brother or sister.

• Support financially organizations that reach out to those in need.

• Form a group of like-minded, compassionate people to share your bounty with those who struggle financially.

Giving Alms to the Poor

Never look down on anyone unless you are helping them up.
ANONYMOUS

Giving alms to the poor encompasses the previous three corporal works of mercy. The following quotations sum up this chapter.

> "When, Lord, did we ever see you hungry and feed you, or thirsty and give you a drink? When did we ever see you a stranger and welcome you in our homes, or naked and clothe you?" The King will reply, "I tell you whenever you did this for one of the least important of these brothers [and sisters) of mine, you did it for me!"
> (MATTHEW 25:37–38, 40)

To the fear of being taken advantage of by someone in need, St. Clement of Alexandria counseled: "You must not try to distinguish between the deserving and the undeserving. You may easily make a mistake, and as the matter is in doubt, it is better to benefit the undeserving than, in avoiding this, to miss the good. We are told not to judge."[9]

In a very moving article, "Hearts Awakened by the Poor," author Jean Vanier writes:

> What does the poor one want? To be loved and recognized as a human person, like you and me, to be loved with a love that is not sentimentality but commitment, understanding, caring—a love that is shown by one's deep desire for the other to be comfortable in body and in being.[10]

FOR REFLECTION AND DISCUSSION

Who inspired you to be a person of compassion? Was it a person you knew or a public figure? Who continues to inspire you?

_____

_____

_____

_____

_____

_____

_____

_____

Jesus tells us to "love our neighbor as ourself." Whom do you understand to be "neighbor"?

_____

_____

_____

_____

_____

_____

_____

_____

Chapter Five

THE CORPORAL WORKS OF MERCY
PART II

*Compassion is language the deaf can hear
and the blind can see.* MARK TWAIN

Visiting the Sick

I must admit, this is the most difficult of the corporal works of mercy for me. Perhaps it goes back to my mother's unsuccessful fight with cancer. It was a two-year struggle for her. I was eighteen and a freshman in college when she was first diagnosed. Whenever I came home for holidays, I saw her in distress. I visited her when she eventually had to be hospitalized. It was very painful for me to see her suffer, though she handled her difficulties with an amazing dignity. I visited her the day before she died. She went to God on Easter Sunday morning in the forty-sixth year of her life.

When my father became ill many years later and I went to visit him in the hospital, I came away in a kind of "shock." I had never seen him really ill before. After I left the hospital, I sought the help of our parish priest, who helped me to deal with my feelings.

So hospital ministry has never appealed to me. But when I have gone—at the request of a family to visit their loved one or from a parish where I have lived—I have found it to be a graced experience not only for the person who is ill but also for me. The sick person, the one facing surgery the following day, the dying one, is Christ in his Passion, his death. I greatly admire those dedicated men and women who bring the Eucharist to the sick on a regular basis, who minister with non-judgmental compassion to those suffering from AIDS or some other serious disease, who serve as live-in caregivers, or who are engaged in hospice. One such person is Nirosh. Here is her story.

> As an extraordinary minister of the Eucharist, I have visited many patients in hospitals on weekends, bringing Holy Communion to the sick and the dying. Some I would visit for months until they either got well or went to God. I was deeply moved by even non-Catholics who would ask to see me; they would

ask, with tear-filled eyes, if I would pray with them.
And I would.

"Visiting the sick" takes many forms, from bringing the Eucharist to praying the Rosary together, to reading a comforting book or just being with the person in their difficult time.[1] In Jesus' life we see his compassion for the sick in his healing ministry, and in one particular case his care for Peter's mother-in-law (Matthew 8:14–15). In verse 16, Matthew sums up Jesus and this corporal work of mercy: "When evening came, people brought to Jesus many who had demons in them. Jesus drove out the evil spirits with a word and healed all who were sick."

Visiting those in Prison
The LORD sets prisoners free and gives sight to the blind.
He lifts those who have fallen. PSALM 146:7–8

One of the themes of Pope Francis' papacy is his encouragement to go beyond our comfort zone and reach out to the most marginalized in society. Here is what he said in a homily on the feast of Pentecost: "The Holy Spirit makes us look to the horizon and drives us to *the very outskirts* [emphasis mine] of existence in order to proclaim life in Jesus Christ."[2] The pope speaks of creating a "culture of friendship" in which we find brothers and sisters made, like us, in the image and likeness of God and who are also children of

God.[3] Visiting those in prison is surely an example of going to the "outskirts."

There are a lot of reasons someone might be in jail or in prison. Here are some:

- Drug-related but nonviolent crime

- More serious offenses, including the capital crime of murder

- White-collar crimes

- For crossing into the United States, or across some other international border, illegally

- As the result of civil disobedience

- wrongly accused or convicted

Regardless of the reason a youth offender or adult is incarcerated, a good question to ask is: "How should I act when I go to visit someone in jail or in prison?" I asked two Catholic priests who have had extensive contact with prisoners for their advice: Fr. Dave Casaleggio and Fr. Brian Highfill.

Fr. Dave, who served at High Desert State Prison in Nevada for a total of fifteen years, emphasized treating men and women "inside" with the same respect you give to those who are not imprisoned. "First of all," he said, "they have the same interpersonal problems that you do—for example, with their families. Second, be aware of your surroundings, don't promise something you can't deliver, and be consistent."

Fr. Brian shared that most of the prisoners he has met suffer from a lack of a sense of self-worth. "They are treated as a number in prison," he said, "which, of course, affects how they see themselves. Bring them hope."[4]

Hope, of course, is what we have for those we meet when visiting them in prison. Hope for his or her emotional and spiritual transformation. Hope that when they are released, they will be able to live a normal life. Hope that someone will give them a second chance and give them a job. In the words of pastor Robert H. Schuller, we hope that the incarcerated one will let their "hopes, not their hurts, shape their future."

Burying the Dead

I performed many charitable works for my kinsmen and my people…If I saw one of my people who had died and been thrown outside the walls of Nineveh, I would bury him.

Toʙɪᴛ 1:16–17 [NAB]

As the *New American Bible* explains, "The Book of Tobit is named for its principal hero. In the story, he is a devout and wealthy Israelite who lives among the captives deported to

Nineveh from the northern kingdom of Israel in 721 BC. He risks his life to bury the dead. Deprivation of burial was viewed with horror by the Jewish people."

Christians believe it is our duty to assist those whose earthly journey is over to have a respectful funeral service and burial. Some reasons are:

- Burial can help the deceased's family and friends to find closure.

- Burial can help with the grieving process.

- Reverence for the deceased's body is essential to honoring this child of God who is a temple of the Holy Spirit.

The *Catechism of the Catholic Church* notes that "The bodies of the dead must be treated with respect and charity, in faith and in the hope of the Resurrection."[5]

The rituals accompanying reverence for the dead include a wake service, the funeral, and the burial of the body or the cremated remains of the deceased at the cemetery.[6] These enable family and friends to pray together for the eternal and peaceful repose of the deceased and give the family of the deceased comfort and consolation. Certainly this was true for our family when my mother died leaving my dad and five children.

Some cultures have additional rituals. For example, the

Irish have given us what is known as "Month's Mind"—a month after the person has died the family comes back to Mass. As one Irish friend put it, "This is a very important part of the grieving process for the family." CatholicIreland. net notes that the Month's Mind "is celebrated in an atmosphere of prayerful remembrance, of gratitude, and of hope in the resurrection. The pain of loss is not as intense now, and the memorial Mass helps us move forward into the future."[7]

In terms of learning how to face the reality of death, I am grateful to the religious sisters who taught me in elementary school not to be afraid of this integral part of the human story. I love this quote from St. Thérèse of Lisieux: "Death is not the horrible specter we see represented in pictures. The catechism teaches that death is the separation of the soul from the body; that is all. I am not afraid of a separation which will unite me forever with God."[8]

A curious thing about this corporal work of mercy concerns the number of people who have experienced "signs" after the death, or burial, from a loved one indicating that the deceased person is okay. I have heard many such stories. Some may say these are merely coincidences—but coincidence is sometimes God's way of remaining anonymous. Here is one such story; it is from Steve, a retired high school coach and teacher.

> Before my Dad died and at his deathbed, he asked me,
> "Stevie, where am I going?" I said, "Dad, you are going

to the peace and to the Light." As he was drifting into death, I told him, "Dad, walk toward the Light." One day, a few weeks later, I was running my usual six miles. At the halfway point, I stopped and asked myself, "I wonder how Dad is doing?" Just then a paper napkin with a star spangled banner on it blew across my feet. It was just like the kind we used at the American Legion building where our family and friends met for the reception after Dad's funeral. But the Legion building was a good ten miles away from where I was standing! I felt a deep peace as I realized this was a sign from Dad that he was okay.

FOR REFLECTION AND DISCUSSION

In Luke 3:22, after Jesus has been baptized by John in the Jordan river, he hears the following from the Father, "You are my beloved Son; with you I am well pleased." This is how God feels about us when we visit the sick or those in prison. Have you ever felt this kind of affirmation? Be open to it.

_____

_____

_____

_____

_____

_____

Does your family or the culture you belong to have any special ways of remembering those family members who have died?

_____

_____

_____

_____

_____

_____

Chapter Six

BEING MERCIFUL TO ONESELF

O Lord, truly you have formed my inmost being;
you knit me in my mother's womb. I give you thanks
that I am fearfully, wonderfully made;
wonderful are your works. Psalm 139:13–14, NAB

People of good will and good heart are sometimes overly hard on themselves in a variety of ways. For example, they might take on too many charitable works at the expense of time with their family, or they might end up neglecting the importance of play in their life. Then there are those who have a difficult time forgiving themselves for some moral transgression. We need to practice acts of mercy to ourselves as well as to others; this is implicit in Jesus' command to "love your neighbor as yourself" (Mark 12:31).

In his Second Letter to the Corinthians, St. Paul, reflecting on liberal giving, writes: "The willingness to give should accord with one's means, not go beyond them. The relief of others ought not to impoverish you" (2 Corinthians 8:12–13, NAB). When I first read this, I thought of it in terms of giving money. But then I applied it to my ministry and saw how it also refers to time and energy. As I get older, my energy is not what it used to be, and my strong work ethic has made it difficult to adjust to this new reality. Two biblical passages that have helped me be more merciful to myself in this regard are in Psalm 23:1–3 and Matthew 11:28–29:

> The LORD is my shepherd;
> I have everything I need.
> He lets me rest in fields of green grass
> and leads me to quiet pools of fresh water.
> He gives me new strength.

> "Come to me, all you who are tired from carrying a
> heavy load and I will give you rest. Take my yoke and
> put it on you, and learn from me, because I am gentle
> and humble in spirit, and you will find rest."

While on one of my own personal retreats, I asked myself, "What do I find restful?" These activities came to mind: listening to classical music, taking walks in the desert near where I live, reading a good novel, spending time with horses—my favorite animal—and having a meal with friends.

How do you find rest?

While writing this book, I asked Robert and Patti Raspo and Ernie and Elaine Seppi—all friends of mine since college, for their ideas on being merciful to oneself. They told me that it is difficult for those who are perfectionists or workaholics to take time off, because their emphasis is on "doing" rather than on "being"; in order to live a balanced life, it is important to have a strong sense of self and not be concerned what other people think of you; as regards being generous, be satisfied with what you can give; and give out of love not from guilt.

I also asked the members of a men's group I belong to in Las Vegas for their ideas on mercy as it relates to one's own life. Two are retired. The others are in business, law, science, and non-profit work. Their responses cover a range of merciful actions:[1]

- "I have learned a lot about self-acceptance, both of my strengths and my weaknesses, from the developmentally disabled men and women I serve."

- "I have come to the conclusion that I want to be the best person I can be, not *the* best, a very freeing place to be."

- "As a way of being kind to myself and to my family I have resigned from two important and prestigious boards in order to spend more time with them."

- "I find it is important to value the spiritual side of life and make time for daily prayer."

- "Giving up the computer and other communication gadgets has given me more time for reading, something I enjoy doing."

- "I discovered that taking time off is not a waste of time, but an investment for tomorrow."

Forgiving Oneself

The effort to forgive oneself, to have mercy on oneself, seems to be a perennial problem. Abbot St. Bernard (1090-1153) encouraged his followers to be confident in the knowledge that when we turn to God in prayer, no matter how great our sins appear, God's kindness is even greater. "Sorrow for sin is indeed necessary," he said, "but it should not be an endless preoccupation."[2] He further encouraged his listeners to "fix their eyes on the aid of the divine mercy."[3]

My own ability to forgive myself for moral transgressions that occurred before I joined the Jesuits was greatly enhanced when I realized one day the unconditional love of God. This was largely due to post-Vatican II theology, where the emphasis has been more on the mercy of God than on judgment. Pope Francis has definitely tapped into this with his emphasis on the "tender mercy of God" rather than on a severe and punishing God.[4] Meditating on Isaiah

43:4 has also greatly helped me: "You are precious in my eyes and glorious and I love you" (NAB).

Terry, who is an accountant in his mid-fifties, shares how he has learned from experience not to be too harsh with himself: "My image of God as kind and loving brought me to find more forgiveness in my heart for myself. I am now better able to accept my shortcomings and find contentment with all the blessings I have been given. An inner peace has come to me over time as I have learned to accept who I am and what is truly important in my life."[5]

Kathy, whose early life image of God was that of a judge, has also found some relief in a newfound experience of God: "Knowing that God knows me as no one else can helps me to be more forgiving of myself, though I still find myself at times falling into my old pattern of trying to meet some impossible moral standard."[6]

Jacques Philippe, who is a French priest and a member of the Community of the Beatitudes, throws further light on the merciful nature of God. The real spiritual battle, he suggests, "consists principally in learning without becoming too discouraged, to accept falling occasionally and not to lose our peace of heart if we should happen to do so lamentably, and placing our interior peace and sense of confident abandonment in the hands of our Father in heaven."[7]

A wonderful meditation that addresses well the journey of self-acceptance and self-forgiveness is called "The Emmaus Road Walk."[8]

First of all, quiet yourself and enter the presence of one who walks with you as a friend: Jesus. Imagine him before you. He asks you to share with him what is troubling you. He wants to share your passion, just as you share his.

In response to this invitation, you tell him about the way you see what is happening to you and how you feel.

Ask him how he feels about you. He reminds you that he is familiar with all your weaknesses as he has been tempted in every way that you have been. Let him accept you where you are. Let him tell you some of the things he appreciates about you, especially in that area of your life where you find yourself most vulnerable. Let him tell you that he loves you most where you love yourself least.

Finally, thank the Lord in some way for his wholehearted acceptance of you. And be at peace.

Loving, caring, and forgiving oneself are not forms of an unhealthy self-indulgence but truly valid ways of honoring one's dignity as a cherished child of God.

FOR REFLECTION AND DISCUSSION

Jesus says, in Matthew 11:28, "Come to me, all you who are tired from carrying heavy loads and I will give you rest." Where do you find rest?

_____

_____

_____

_____

_____

_____

_____

On forgiving yourself: Do you find this easy to do? If not, what do you think the resistance is?

_____

_____

_____

_____

_____

_____

_____

_____

Conclusion

The virtue of mercy is needed more than ever today. This is true not only within the Catholic Church and its renewed emphasis on forgiveness over judgment but also in the wider human community and in respect to the planet on which we live. We are living in a time when the values of the West are under attack from sinister forces. Even larger than that are the threats to the Earth. In addition to the seven spiritual and seven corporal works of mercy, which we have reflected on in this book, it would seem appropriate to add a work of mercy for the environment: *serious commitment to saving our common home*. Pope Francis, in his encyclical letter *Laudato Si'*, clearly points us in this direction. Writes the pope: "The urgent challenge to protect our common home includes a concern to bring the whole human family together to seek a sustainable and integral development, for we know that things can change" (no. 13).

Forgiving those who have harmed us or sought to harm us or those we love is a major challenge to living the virtue of mercy. Normally, it takes time and patience and a lot of grace to do it. I know this from my own experience. But if we can't do this on an interpersonal level, how can we expect nations to do it?

Pope Francis is to be admired and thanked for bringing the virtue of mercy more fully into both church and public discourse. As a Catholic priest, I have been more aware of the soul-soothing effect of acting mercifully in the confessional because of the Jubilee Year of Mercy. May the greater awareness of this important virtue continue to deepen and grow during the Jubilee Year and beyond.

MERCY AND THE MASS

Divine Mercy
Lamb of God
and shepherd of our souls.
You forgive and heal us
when we ask with true humility
for your merciful grace.

You take away the sins of the world
and forgive us our trespasses
as you ask us to forgive others theirs.
Continue to shower your mercy upon us
that with your help we may reach out in mercy
to those most in need of your grace.

Help us, as we receive you in the Eucharist
to be food for our hungry world
by living the spiritual and corporal works of mercy
in imitation of you
with
your compassion and courage.

As your disciples, may our prayer
and our actions
further and deepen
the reign of God
now
and unto the life yet to come.
Amen.

Notes

CHAPTER ONE

1. *The Modern Catholic Encyclopedia*, edited by Michael Glazer and Monika Hellwig (Collegeville, MN: The Liturgical Press, 1994), pp. 562–563.

2. *The Merchant of Venice*, Act IV, Scene I, by William Shakespeare.

3. See also Psalm 86:1–5.

4. Some translations have "in truth" or "with integrity" instead of "with sincerity."

5. Elizabeth Fry, in *The Flowering of the Soul: A Book of Prayers by Women*, edited by Lucinda Vardey (Boston, MA: Beacon Press, 1999), p. 252. Used with permission.

6. Saint Pope John Paul II, *Rich in Mercy* (November 30, 1980), no. 2.

7.   Pope Francis, *The Church of Mercy* (Chicago, IL: Loyola Press, 2014). The quote is from the Foreword (p. ix) and is by Vincent Cardinal Nichols, Archbishop of Westminster and head of the Roman Catholic Church in England and Wales.

8   Pope Francis, *The Church of Mercy*, p. viii.

9.   Saint John Paul II, *Rich in Mercy*, no. 6.

10.   Pope Francis, *The Church of Mercy*, p. 3.

11.   Pope Francis, *The Church of Mercy*, p. 3.

12.   *Catechism of the Catholic Church*, no. 2447.

13.   James F. Keenan, SJ, *Moral Wisdom: Lessons and Texts from the Catholic Tradition* (Lanham, MD: A Sheed and Ward Book, Rowan and Littlefield, 2004), p. 124.

CHAPTER TWO

1.   *The Documents of Vatican II*, "Pastoral Constitution on the Church in the Modern World," no. 27; General Editor Walter M. Abbott, SJ (New York, New York: The America Press, 1966).

2. Pope Francis, *The Church of Mercy*, p. 81.

3. James F. Keenan, SJ, *Moral Wisdom: Lessons and Texts from the Catholic Tradition*, p. 129.

4. Saint John Paul II, *Rich in Mercy*, no. 6.

5. John Shea, *The Challenge of Jesus* (Thomas More Press, 1984). Quoted in *The Living Pulpit*, April-June, 1994, p. 30. This story is in Luke 19:1–10.

6. Pope Francis, *Misericordiae Vultus* (Bull of Indiction of the Extraordinary Jubilee of Mercy), 11 April, 2015, no. 4.

7. *Give Us This Day*, June 2015, p. 243.

8. George Herbert lived from 1593–1633.

9. Robert Spitzer, SJ, *The Spirit of Leadership* (Provo, Utah: Executive Excellence Publishing, 2000), pp. 227–28.

10. Mary E. Hunt, "To Forgive or not to Forgive?" *Living Pulpit* (April-June, 1994), pp. 14–15.

11. Henri J. M. Nouwen, "Forgiveness: The Name of Love in a Wounded World," *Weavings* (March/April, 1992), p. 14.

12. Carolyn Osiek, RSCJ, *Beyond Anger: On Being a Feminist in the Church* (Mahwah, NJ: Paulist Press, 1986).

13. Quoted in "A Brother Whom I Have Pardoned," by Walter Burghardt, SJ, *Living Pulpit* (April-June, 1994), pp. 10-11. The quote is originally from *Time* Magazine, January 19, 1984.

14. Lewis B. Smedes, *Forgive and Forget: Healing the Hurts We Don't Deserve* (New York, NY: Simon & Schuster Pocket Books, 1984), p. 153. See also my book, *The Masculine Spirit: Resources for Reflective Living* (Notre Dame, IN: Ave Maria Press, 1997), Chapter 7 "Dealing with Father Wounds."

CHAPTER THREE

1. Mark P. Shea, "Bear Wrongs Patiently." www.catholiccity. com (July 13, 2010), p. 2.

2. Steve Garvey, "The Passion of Jackie Robinson" in *My Bat Boy Days: Lessons I Learned from the Boys of Summer* (New York, NY: Scribner, Simon and Schuster, 2008), pp. 51-69. This is a gem of a book, both heartwarming and inspiring as the author shares reflections on nine baseball greats. See also Jackie Robinson's autobiography, *I Never Had It Made* (various editions, originally published by Putnam Publishing Group in 1972).

3. Garvey, *My Bat Boy Days*, p. 54.

4. Garvey, *My Bat Boy Days*, pp. 60-61.

5. See Chapter 7 on the Seventh Commandment, "You shall not steal," in my book *The 10 Commandments for Everyday Life* (Toronto: Novalis, 2015).

6. See Appendix C in my book *Beatitudes for the Workplace* (Toronto: Novalis, 2009) for a six-step process for using your imagination in praying about Jesus.

7. Richard M. Gula, SS, *Reason Informed by Faith: Foundations of Catholic Morality* (Mahwah, NJ: Paulist Press, 1989), pp. 116-121. This is an excellent treatment of social sin—"The notion of social sin articulates how social structures can shape our experience for the worse; wherein people suffer various forms of oppression and exploitation" (p. 116).

8. Donald P. McNeill, Douglas A. Morrison, and Henri Nouwen, *Compassion: A Reflection on the Christian Life* (New York, NY: Image Books, 1983), p. 4.

9. Oliva, *Beatitudes for the Workplace*, pp. 73-76. Two of my conversion to compassion experiences are described here: in the African American community, and in relation to homosexual men.

10. Frederick Buechner, *Peculiar Treasures* (San Francisco, HarperOne, 1993).

11. Pope Francis, *Misericordiae Vultus* ("The Face of Mercy"), no. 4.

12. Pope Francis, *The Church of Mercy,* p. 66.

13. Karen Jaenke, "AIDS Ministry," *Fellowship in Prayer* (now known as *Sacred Journey*) (October, 1988), p. 32.

14. Angela Alaimo O'Donnell, "In Our Sons' Names," *America* (May 18, 2015), p. 41.

15. Carl F. Smith, *Special Love: A Gift in a Damaged Package* (CreateSpace Independent Publishing, 2014; available from Amazon). This book will leave you questioning what really constitutes a disability and how, although minds and bodies can be handicapped, the heart's ability to heal, learn, and develop is limitless.

16. J. Kevin Appleby, "The Migrant Pope," *America* (July 6-13, 2015), p. 26.

17. Appleby, "The Migrant Pope," p. 27.

18. Ann Dawson, *A Season of Grief* (Notre Dame, IN: Ave Maria Press, 2002), pp. 19-20. Adapted for this chapter.

CHAPTER FOUR

1. See also Mark 8:1–9.

2. See my book *Beatitudes for the Workplace*, Chapter Four, for a full treatment of what I have learned by immersing myself in other cultures.

3. In *Praying the Beatitudes* (Dublin, Ireland: Veritas, 1990), Chapter One, I wrote about my time in Calcutta.

4. Pope Francis, *The Church of Mercy*, p. xii.

5. Pope Francis, *The Church of Mercy*, p. 18.

6. The full poem is called, "To Althea from Prison" and was written by Richard Lovelace in 1642.

7. Future in Humanity is located at: 215 N. Lemon St., Fullerton, Ca. 92832, futureinhumanity.org.

8. Mark Shea, "Clothe the Naked: Acknowledging the Need for Human Dignity," *National Catholic Register*, ncregister.com/daily-news/clothe-the-naked-acknowledging-the-need-for-human-dignity.

9. "Quis Dives Salvetur?" Translated in R.B. Tollinton, Clement of Alexandria, 318.

10.   As quoted in *Sojourners*, January, 1982.

CHAPTER FIVE

1.   A resource I have found helpful for this corporal work of
     mercy is: *How Can I Help?* by Ram Dass and Paul Gorman
     (New York, NY: Alfred A. Knopf, 1985), especially chapters
     three and four.

2.   Pope Francis, *The Church of Mercy*, p. 49.

3.   Pope Francis, *The Church of Mercy*, p. 100.

4.   An excellent additional resource is "The Do's and Don'ts of
     Volunteer Prison Visits," published online by Prison
     Fellowship, Dec. 3, 2009.

5.   *Catechism of the Catholic Church*, no. 2300. See also *Funerals:
     A Guide*, by James Bentley, Andrew Best & Jackie Hunt
     (London, England: Hodder and Stoughton, 1995).

6.   *Catechism of the Catholic Church*, no. 2301; on cremation.

7.   "Celebrating a life through liturgy," 30 November 1999.
     CatholicIreland.net

8.   Thérèse of Lisieux, "Counsels and Reminiscences."

CHAPTER SIX

1. The members are: Bob Brown, Joe Brown, Chester Clagett, Steve Curtis, Jim Lamb, John Laub, Dominic Marrocco, Tom Mazelin, and Ross Williams.

2. "Jesus the Physician," by Fr. Paul Murray, OP, *Magnificat* (August 31, 2015), p. 434.

3. Murray, "Jesus the Physician," p. 435.

4. Pope Francis, *The Church of Mercy*, p. 31.

5. Max Oliva, S.J., *God of Many Loves* (Notre Dame, IN: Ave Maria Press, 2001), p. 46.

6. Oliva, *God of Many Loves*, p. 46.

7. "Neither do I condemn you," by Jacques Philippe, *Magnificat* (March 23, 2015), pp. 357-358.

8. Peter Hannan, SJ, *Nine Faces of God* (Dublin, Ireland: The Columba Press, 1992), pp. 29-30. See also *How to Forgive Yourself and Others*, by Fr. Eamon Tobin (Liguori, Missouri: Liguori Publications, 1993).

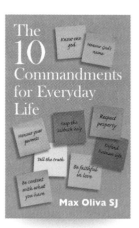
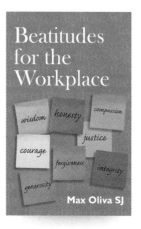